The Apocalypse of Abraham

Visions of Faith, Judgment, and Di-vine Mysteries

A Modern Translation

Adapted for the Contemporary Reader

Abraham the Patriarch

Translated by Tim Zengerink

© **Copyright 2025**
All rights reserved.

It is not legal to reproduce, duplicate, or transmit any part of this document in either electronic means or in printed format. Recording of this publication is strictly prohibited and any storage of this document is not allowed unless with written permission from the publisher except for the use of brief quotations in a book review.

This book contains works of fiction. Any resemblance to persons living or dead, or places, events, or locations is purely coincidental.

Table Of Contents

Preface - Message to the Reader 1

Introduction 5

The Apocalypse of Abraham 11

Thank You for Reading 26

Preface - Message to the Reader

What If You Could Help Rebuild the Greatest Library in Human History?

Thousands of years ago, the Library of Alexandria stood as the crown jewel of human achievement — a sanctuary where the collected wisdom of every known civilization was gathered, preserved, and shared freely.

And then, it was lost.

Through fire, conquest, and the slow erosion of time, humanity lost not just books — but ideas, dreams, discoveries, and stories that could have changed the world forever.

Today, the Library of Alexandria lives again — and you are invited to be a part of its restoration.

Our mission is simple yet profound:

To rebuild the greatest library the world has ever known, and to translate all timeless works into every language and dialect, so that no seeker of knowledge is ever left behind again.

By joining our movement to rebuild the modern Library of Alexandria, you become part of an unprecedented mission:

- **Unlimited Access to the Greatest Audiobooks & eBooks Ever Written:**

    Instantly explore thousands of legendary works—Plato, Shakespeare, Jane Austen, Leo Tolstoy, and countless more. All instantly available to read or listen, placing a complete literary universe at your fingertips.

- **Beautiful Paperback & Deluxe Editions at Printing Cost**

    Own any title as an elegant paperback, deluxe hardcover, or stunning collectible boxset—offered to you at true printing cost, delivered straight to your door. Build your personal Library of Alexandria, crafted for beauty, built for durability, and worthy of proud display.

- **Fresh Translations for Modern Readers—in Every Language & Dialect**

    Enjoy timeless masterpieces reimagined in clear, contemporary language—no more outdated phrases or obscure references. Alongside the original versions, we're tirelessly translating these classics into every language and dialect imaginable, ensuring accessibility and understanding across cultures and generations.

- **Join a Global Renaissance of Literature & Knowledge**

    You directly support expanding our library, publishing deluxe editions at true cost, translating works into all global languages, and bringing humanity's greatest stories to people everywhere. By joining today, you're not just preserving a legacy of masterpieces; you set in motion a powerful wave of literary accessibility.

Become a Torchbearer of Knowledge.

Join us for free now at **LibraryofAlexandria.com**

Together, we will ensure that the light of human wisdom never fades again.

With gratitude and a shared love of knowledge,

The Modern Library of Alexandria Team

Visit:

www.libraryofalexandria.com

Or scan the code below:

Introduction

The Patriarch's Vision and the Path to Divine Wisdom

The Apocalypse of Abraham stands as one of the most evocative and spiritually rich apocalyptic texts from the Second Temple period, offering a unique window into the religious imagination of ancient Judaism and its engagement with themes of divine revelation, cosmic order, and human destiny. Attributed to Abraham—the patriarch revered across Judaism, Christianity, and Islam—this visionary work transcends tradition and invites modern readers into a profound encounter with the mysteries of faith, judgment, and divine purpose. In a world increasingly distanced from sacred mystery, this ancient text speaks with renewed urgency, offering timeless insight into the soul's relationship with the divine and the unfolding drama of good and evil within creation.

Unlike other apocalyptic texts that emerge from communities under political or religious oppression, The Apocalypse of Abraham begins with a highly personal and intimate story: Abraham's rejection of idolatry and his awakening to the call of the Most High.

The narrative then shifts dramatically as Abraham is chosen to ascend into the heavenly realms and receive visions of cosmic scale. Guided by the angel Yahoel, a celestial being of immense power and holiness, Abraham journeys beyond the physical world to witness the structure of creation, the forces that shape it, and the fate of all that dwells within. Through this ascent, Abraham is not only transformed himself but also positioned as a witness to the divine order—an emissary between the sacred and the human.

What sets The Apocalypse of Abraham apart from other ancient revelations is its fusion of personal transformation and cosmic vision. The text blends rich symbolism, liturgical motifs, and apocalyptic prophecy into a singular narrative that explores the origin of evil, the role of Satan (referred to as Azazel), and the final judgment of humanity. This is not simply a story about Abraham's past but a meditation on universal themes: What does it mean to trust God in a broken world? How is divine justice ultimately revealed? What role do humans play in the eternal struggle between light and darkness? These questions resonate far beyond the ancient world, inviting every reader to examine their own journey of faith.

Abraham's encounter with the divine begins with destruction—the smashing of idols, the death of his father, and the burning of falsehood. This rupture with the past is essential for the revelation to come. Only when the illusions of the world are shattered can the truth of the divine be revealed. Abraham's courage to walk away from tradition, to question authority, and to seek the voice of the unseen God is the first step in a journey that leads him beyond the stars. This theme of renunciation as preparation for revelation is central to the text's spiritual message. The reader is invited to consider what illusions must be surrendered in their own life in order to see clearly and hear truly.

The angel Yahoel, who guides Abraham through the heavens, serves not only as a protector but as a model of holiness—bearing the ineffable name of God and displaying perfect obedience to the divine will. His presence introduces a mystical dimension to the narrative, linking the earthly and celestial, and prefiguring the angelic mediators found in later mystical traditions. The dialogue between Abraham and Yahoel is marked by awe, reverence, and growing understanding. It models a spiritual relationship in which the seeker is led, instructed, and ultimately empowered to see what is normally hidden. Through this sacred companionship, Abraham learns not only the secrets of the cosmos but the nature of God's justice and mercy.

Cosmic Struggle, Judgment, and the Role of Faith

As Abraham ascends, he witnesses the structure of the heavens, the angelic hierarchies, and the unfolding history of humanity. He sees the division between the righteous and the wicked, the corruption introduced by Azazel, and the final restoration of divine order. These visions are not abstract theology but moral revelation: they teach that every soul stands within a vast spiritual conflict, and that choices made in this life echo through eternity. The struggle is not merely external; it is internal. Azazel, the fallen one, does not only corrupt the world—he tempts the soul. The apocalypse reveals that salvation is not only about divine intervention but about personal integrity, resistance to evil, and unwavering faith in the unseen.

The figure of Azazel is central to the text's understanding of evil. Cast as both tempter and accuser, he reflects the dual nature of evil as both seductive and destructive. His domain is the earth, yet his influence stretches across the heavens. He represents not just chaos but rebellion—an intelligence turned against the divine order. Abraham is shown the effects of Azazel's influence: wars, idolatry, injustice, and despair. Yet the vision also affirms that Azazel's power is temporary, and that divine justice will prevail. The faithful will be vindicated, the righteous will be gathered, and the world will be restored to harmony.

In this cosmic vision, Abraham also sees the coming of a chosen one—a messianic figure who will play a central role in the final judgment and the restoration of creation. This element links The Apocalypse of Abraham with broader messianic expectations of the Second Temple period and offers a vision of hope grounded not in fantasy but in the certainty of divine purpose. The messianic figure is not detailed at length, but his presence affirms that history has direction, that justice is not an illusion, and that the divine plan is unfolding even in the midst of suffering.

The final scenes of the apocalypse reveal Abraham in awe before the glory of God. He is shown the heavenly temple, the light of the divine presence, and the coming judgment. He is instructed to share his vision—not as prophecy alone, but as invitation. The message of The Apocalypse of Abraham is not only that God speaks, but that God calls each soul to respond. Faith, in this context, is not blind belief but courageous trust: the willingness to see beyond appearances, to walk in obedience, and to hold fast to the vision of truth in a world of shadows.

This modern translation seeks to render the full force of this ancient text in language that speaks to contemporary readers while preserving the poetic cadence, reverent tone, and symbolic depth of the original. It is a spiritual document, not a historical artifact. Every image, every phrase, every vision is meant to awaken—not just the mind, but the heart. It is not written to be analyzed alone, but to be meditated upon, to be lived.

To read The Apocalypse of Abraham is to be drawn into a sacred journey—a journey that begins in doubt, passes through revelation, and arrives at trust. It is a story of one man's ascent into the mysteries of God, but it is also the story of every soul that longs to know why we are here, where we are going, and what truth lies beyond the veil. It does not give easy answers, but it gives lasting hope. In a world of confusion, it offers clarity. In a world of despair, it offers vision. In a world of silence, it offers the voice of the Most High.

Let this book accompany you into the deeper chambers of your own faith. Let Abraham's questions become your own. Let his visions challenge your assumptions. And let his unwavering trust in the face of the unknown inspire you to walk your own path of revelation—with open eyes, with a steady heart, and with a spirit ready to receive the mysteries of the divine.

The Apocalypse of Abraham

Abraham was known for his kindness, fairness, and generosity. He lived near a place called Dria the Black, at a crossroads where many travelers passed through. He welcomed everyone—rich or poor, kings or commoners, strong or weak. No matter who they were, Abraham treated them with kindness because he was a good and just man who loved people.

One day, the Lord called the archangel Michael and said, "Go to my servant Abraham and remind him that his time on earth is coming to an end. I have blessed him greatly, making his descendants as countless as the stars in the sky and the sand on the shore. He has lived a life full of goodness and generosity. Now, his time has come."

Michael, who sat before the Lord, left heaven and went to find Abraham in Dria the Black. When he arrived, he saw Abraham working in the field with his servants and some young men. The archangel approached him and said, "Greetings, honored father, chosen one of the Lord, beloved friend of the King of Heaven."

Abraham replied, "Greetings to you, mighty one of God's army! You are more radiant than any man I have ever seen. Tell me, young man, where do you come from, and why do you shine so brightly?"

Michael answered, "Righteous Abraham, I come from the Great City. The Great King has sent me to His chosen friend to tell him to prepare himself, for the Lord is calling him."

Abraham nodded and said, "Very well. Let us go back to my home." Then he called his servants and said, "Go to the field and bring two of my horses. Prepare them so I may ride one, and my guest may ride the other."

But Michael replied, "Do not bring the horses. I do not ride animals with four legs. Let us walk together, righteous one."

As they walked, they passed by a tall and sturdy cypress tree. Suddenly, the tree cried out, "The Lord calls you, Abraham!" But Abraham remained silent, unsure if the angel had heard it.

When they reached Abraham's home, they sat down. Isaac, Abraham's son, saw the angel and said to his mother, Sarah, "Look at the man sitting with my father. He does not look like any ordinary person."

Isaac ran to the angel, bowed before him, and the angel blessed him, saying, "May God give you all the blessings He has given to your father and mother."

Abraham turned to Isaac and said, "Bring a basin and fill it with water so we can wash our guest's feet."

Isaac ran to the well, filled a basin, and brought it back. As Abraham washed the angel's feet, he sighed deeply and began to cry. Seeing his father weep, Isaac also started to cry, and their tears fell together. The angel, moved by their sadness, wept as well. As his tears fell into the basin, they turned into precious stones.

When Abraham saw this, he gathered the jewels and kept their meaning in his heart.

Then Abraham told his son, "Go prepare two beds carefully. Set candles in the candlesticks, lay out the table, light incense, and spread fragrant herbs on the floor so the room smells sweet. Light seven candles so that we may celebrate this guest, who is greater than any man and mightier than kings."

Isaac did everything as his father instructed.

Abraham and the angel went into the prepared room. They sat down on separate beds with a table of food between them. Then the angel returned to the Lord and said, "Lord, I have seen Abraham's righteousness, kindness, and incredible strength. I cannot bring myself to tell him about his approaching death because I have never met anyone like him on earth."

The Lord replied, "Go back to my friend Abraham. Eat the food he has prepared, and I will send My Spirit to his son Isaac. In a dream, I will reveal to him that his father's time is near. You will interpret the dream so that Abraham may understand that his time has come."

The archangel said, "Lord, heavenly beings do not eat or drink. How can I sit and eat with Abraham?"

The Lord replied, "Do not worry. I will send spirits to make the food disappear from your hands and mouth, as if you were eating. This will bring joy to Abraham and his family. Also, explain Isaac's dream so they understand what is about to happen."

The archangel returned to Abraham, and they ate together. As usual, Abraham said a prayer before the meal. After eating, they prayed again and then rested on their beds.

Isaac turned to his father and said, "I want to stay here and listen to our guest."

But Abraham replied, "No, my son. Go to bed and rest. We must not trouble our guest."

Isaac obeyed, received his father's blessing, and went to his room.

Later that night, Isaac had a dream that frightened him. He ran to his father's room, where Abraham was still with the archangel, and cried, "Father Abraham, please open the door! Let me hold you before they take you away from me!"

Abraham got up and opened the door. Isaac ran inside, embraced his father, and wept loudly. Abraham also wept, and when the archangel saw them, he wept too.

Abraham gently asked Isaac, "My dear son, tell me what you saw in your dream that has upset you so much."

Isaac replied, "I saw the sun and the moon resting on my head, shining brightly in all directions. At first, I was happy, but then the heavens opened, and a glowing man came down. He removed the sun from my head and took it to heaven. Then he did the same with the moon. I begged him, 'Please, do not take them away from me!' But he said, 'Let them go. The Lord of Heaven has called for them.' Although they left some of their light behind, I felt heartbroken."

Abraham sighed and said, "The sun you saw, and the glowing man from heaven, must mean that my time to leave has come." He then turned to the angel and said, "Oh, how amazing! But I fear you are the one who has come to take my soul from me."

The archangel replied, "I am the angel sent to bring you news of your passing. You will go to the Lord as promised in your covenant."

Abraham answered, "Now I understand that you are here to take my soul, but I will not go willingly!"

The angel returned to the Lord and reported everything that had happened, including Abraham's refusal, saying, "He will not surrender."

The Lord said to the archangel, "Go back to my friend Abraham and remind him: I am the Lord, his God, who led him to the Promised Land. I blessed him with descendants as countless as the sand on the shore and the stars in the sky. How dare he resist me? Does he not know that since the time of Adam and Eve, all people have died? Kings, ancestors, and all of humanity have faced death because no one is immortal.

"But I have not sent him sickness, suffering, or the grim reaper to take him away. Instead, I sent my archangel Michael with this message so Abraham could prepare himself. Why does he resist my messenger? Does he not know I could send the angel of death, whose presence he could not endure?"

The archangel returned to Abraham and repeated the Lord's words. Abraham wept and said, "Mighty angel of heaven, though I am a sinner, you have honored me. Please grant me one last request. The Lord has always answered my prayers and given me what I asked for. I know I cannot escape death, but before I die, let me see all the people of the earth and their deeds while I am still alive. After that, I will surrender myself completely."

The archangel returned to heaven and told the Lord about Abraham's request.

The Lord said, "Place my servant Abraham in the chariot of the cherubim and bring him up to heaven."

Then sixty angels prepared the chariot. Abraham was lifted up on the clouds. As he traveled, he saw another chariot behind him and groups of people below.

In one area, he saw people committing terrible sins and cried out, "Lord, let the earth open and swallow them!"

In another place, he saw people stealing and harming others and shouted, "Lord, send fire from heaven to destroy them!"

Fire came down and consumed them.

A voice from heaven commanded, "Take Abraham away from this sight so he will not see the people any longer. If he continues watching their sins, he will destroy them all. But I do not wish for anyone to perish. I want the wicked to repent and live. Take Abraham to the first gate of heaven so he may witness the final judgment and humble himself even more."

The archangel turned Abraham's chariot and brought him to the first gate of heaven. There, he saw two paths—one narrow and difficult, the other wide and easy.

On the narrow path, only a few souls were walking, each guided by an angel.

On the wide path, there were many souls, but they looked wounded and suffering, being led by different beings.

Then Abraham noticed a powerful figure sitting on a golden throne. Sometimes, the figure wept, pulling at his hair and beard when he saw the many souls on the wide path. Other times, he rejoiced when he saw the few souls walking the narrow path.

Abraham turned to the archangel and asked, "Who is this man who switches between sorrow and joy?"

The archangel answered, "This is Adam, the first man, created to bring beauty to the world. He rejoices when he sees souls on the narrow path because it leads to life. But when he sees so many souls on the wide path, which leads to destruction, he mourns deeply."

As they spoke, two angels arrived, bringing countless souls before Adam. Some were sent down the narrow path, while others were turned away.

Then Abraham saw another golden throne at a large gateway. It shined like fire, and a man sat on it, resembling the Son of God. In front of him was a massive table, and two angels stood beside him.

One angel held a set of scales, and the other held a scroll listing all the temptations and sins of humanity. The man judged each soul, deciding their fate.

The angel on the right recorded virtues, while the angel on the left noted sins. Some souls were condemned, others were set free, and a few were placed in the middle.

Abraham asked the archangel, "What is this I see before me?"

The angel replied, "These are the judges, and they pass judgment on every soul that comes before them."

Abraham watched as one soul was brought forward.

An angel said, "This soul has an equal number of good and bad deeds. Erase its record, for it will neither be saved nor condemned. Place it in the middle."

Abraham then asked, "Who are these judges and the glowing angels surrounding them?"

The archangel said, "Lord, heavenly beings do not eat or drink. How can I sit and eat with Abraham?"

The Lord replied, "Do not worry. I will send spirits

to make the food disappear from your hands and mouth, as if you were eating. This will bring joy to Abraham and his family. Also, explain Isaac's dream so they understand what is about to happen."

The archangel returned to Abraham, and they ate together. As usual, Abraham said a prayer before the meal. After eating, they prayed again and then rested on their beds.

Isaac turned to his father and said, "I want to stay here and listen to our guest."

But Abraham replied, "No, my son. Go to bed and rest. We must not trouble our guest."

Isaac obeyed, received his father's blessing, and went to his room.

Later that night, Isaac had a dream that frightened him. He ran to his father's room, where Abraham was still with the archangel, and cried, "Father Abraham, please open the door! Let me hold you before they take you away from me!"

Abraham got up and opened the door. Isaac ran inside, embraced his father, and wept loudly. Abraham also wept, and when the archangel saw them, he wept too.

Abraham gently asked Isaac, "My dear son, tell me what you saw in your dream that has upset you so much."

Isaac replied, "I saw the sun and the moon resting on my head, shining brightly in all directions. At first, I was happy, but then the heavens opened, and a glowing man came down. He removed the sun from my head and took it to heaven. Then he did the same with the moon. I begged him, 'Please, do not take them away from me!' But he said, 'Let them go. The Lord of Heaven has called for them.' Although they left some of their light behind, I felt heartbroken."

Abraham sighed and said, "The sun you saw, and the glowing man from heaven, must mean that my time to leave has come." He then turned to the angel and said, "Oh, how amazing! But I fear you are the one who has come to take my soul from me."

The archangel replied, "I am the angel sent to bring you news of your passing. You will go to the Lord as promised in your covenant."

Abraham answered, "Now I understand that you are here to take my soul, but I will not go willingly!"

The angel returned to the Lord and reported everything that had happened, including Abraham's refusal, saying, "He will not surrender."

The Lord said to the archangel, "Go back to my friend Abraham and remind him: I am the Lord, his God, who led him to the Promised Land. I blessed him with descendants as countless as the sand on the shore and the stars in the sky. How dare he resist me? Does he not know that since the time of Adam and Eve, all people have died? Kings, ancestors, and all of humanity have faced death because no one is immortal.

"But I have not sent him sickness, suffering, or the grim reaper to take him away. Instead, I sent my archangel Michael with this message so Abraham could prepare himself. Why does he resist my messenger? Does he not know I could send the angel of death, whose presence he could not endure?"

The archangel returned to Abraham and repeated the Lord's words. Abraham wept and said, "Mighty angel of heaven, though I am a sinner, you have honored me. Please grant me one last request. The Lord has always answered my prayers and given me what I asked for. I know I cannot escape death, but before I die, let me see all the people of the earth and their deeds while I am still alive. After that, I will surrender myself completely."

The archangel returned to heaven and told the Lord about Abraham's request.

The Lord said, "Place my servant Abraham in the chariot of the cherubim and bring him up to heaven."

Then sixty angels prepared the chariot. Abraham was lifted up on the clouds. As he traveled, he saw another chariot behind him and groups of people below.

In one area, he saw people committing terrible sins and cried out, "Lord, let the earth open and swallow them!"

In another place, he saw people stealing and harming others and shouted, "Lord, send fire from heaven to destroy them!"

Fire came down and consumed them.

A voice from heaven commanded, "Take Abraham away from this sight so he will not see the people any longer. If he continues watching their sins, he will destroy them all. But I do not wish for anyone to perish. I want the wicked to repent and live. Take Abraham to the first gate of heaven so he may witness the final judgment and humble himself even more."

The archangel turned Abraham's chariot and brought him to the first gate of heaven. There, he saw two paths—one narrow and difficult, the other wide and easy.

On the narrow path, only a few souls were walking, each guided by an angel.

On the wide path, there were many souls, but they looked wounded and suffering, being led by different beings.

Then Abraham noticed a powerful figure sitting on a golden throne. Sometimes, the figure wept, pulling at his hair and beard when he saw the many souls on the wide path. Other times, he rejoiced when he saw the few souls walking the narrow path.

Abraham turned to the archangel and asked, "Who is this man who switches between sorrow and joy?"

The archangel answered, "This is Adam, the first man, created to bring beauty to the world. He rejoices when he sees souls on the narrow path because it leads to life. But when he sees so many souls on the wide path, which leads to destruction, he mourns deeply."

As they spoke, two angels arrived, bringing countless souls before Adam. Some were sent down the narrow path, while others were turned away.

Then Abraham saw another golden throne at a large gateway. It shined like fire, and a man sat on it, resembling the Son of God. In front of him was a massive table, and two angels stood beside him.

One angel held a set of scales, and the other held a scroll listing all the temptations and sins of humanity. The man judged each soul, deciding their fate.

The angel on the right recorded virtues, while the angel on the left noted sins. Some souls were condemned, others were set free, and a few were placed in the middle.

Abraham asked the archangel, "What is this I see

before me?"

The angel replied, "These are the judges, and they pass judgment on every soul that comes before them."

Abraham watched as one soul was brought forward.

An angel said, "This soul has an equal number of good and bad deeds. Erase its record, for it will neither be saved nor condemned. Place it in the middle."

Abraham then asked, "Who are these judges and the glowing angels surrounding them?"

Thank You for Reading

Dear Reader,

We hope this timeless classic has sparked your imagination and enriched your literary journey. Now that you've turned the final page, we want to share a vision for the future of reading—one where every classic you've ever wanted to explore is at your fingertips, in a format that best suits your life.

We'd like to invite you to gain immediate, unlimited digital & audiobook access to hundreds of the most treasured literary classics ever written—along with the option to secure deluxe paperback, hardcover & box set editions at printing cost. Together, we can spark a new global literary renaissance alongside our small, independent publishing house called "The Library of Alexandria."

Thousands of years ago, the Library of Alexandria stood as a beacon of knowledge—until it was lost to history. We aim to reignite that spirit of preservation and discovery right now, in the modern age—only this time, it's accessible to all, in every language and every format.

Picture a world where every timeless classic, novel, poem, or philosophical treatise is not only available to read but also updated for today's readers—modernized, translated into any language or dialect, and ready to enjoy in any format you choose, whether that is in an eBook, audiobook, paperback, or deluxe hardcover & box set version a printing cost.

By joining our movement to rebuild the modern Library of Alexandria, you become part of an unprecedented mission to offer:

- **Unlimited Audiobook & eBook Access to the Greatest Classics of All Time**

  Instantly explore thousands of legendary works, from Plato and Shakespeare to Jane Austen and Leo Tolstoy. All are instantly ready to read or listen to, giving you a complete literary universe at your fingertips.

- **Paperback & Deluxe Editions at Printing Costs:**

  Purchase any title in a paperback, deluxe hardbound, or deluxe boxset edition at printing costs, shipped right to your doorstep. Curate your personal library of Alexandria with editions worthy of display—crafted to last, designed to captivate, and delivered straight to your door.

- **Modern translations for Contemporary Readers in all languages and dialects**

    Discover a vast selection of classics reimagined in clear, current language—no more struggling with outdated phrases or obscure references. Next to the original versions, we aim to offer translations in as many languages and dialects as possible.

    As we continue our translation efforts and add new languages, readers everywhere can connect with these works as if they were written today. By bridging linguistic divides, you're contributing to ensuring that these timeless stories become more meaningful, accessible, and inspiring for people across the globe.

- **Your Personal Library of Alexandria:**

    Over the months and years, you'll curate a unique physical archive of classics—each volume a testament to your taste, curiosity, and love of knowledge. It's not just about owning books—it's about curating a cultural legacy you'll cherish and pass down for generations to come.

- **Join a Global Literary Renaissance:**

    Your support fuels an ongoing mission: allowing us to reinvest in offering deluxe print editions (including special boxsets) at their true cost, broaden the range of available formats and translations, and extend the reach of these works to new audiences worldwide. By joining today, you're not just preserving a legacy of masterpieces; you set in motion a powerful wave of literary accessibility.

We are more than a publisher—we're a movement, and we can't do it alone. Your support lets us scale our mission, preserving and reimagining history's greatest works for tomorrow's readers.

Become a Torchbearer of knowledge.

Thank you for picking up this book and allowing us into your literary journey. As you turn the pages, know that you're part of something larger: a global effort to keep these stories alive, share their wisdom across borders and generations, and spark a true cultural revival for the modern era.

If this resonates with you—please consider taking the next step by visiting:

www.libraryofalexandria.com

With gratitude and a shared love of knowledge,

The Modern Library of Alexandria Team

Visit:

www.libraryofalexandria.com

Or scan the code below:

www.ingramcontent.com/pod-product-compliance
Lightning Source LLC
LaVergne TN
LVHW030631080426
835512LV00021B/3463